The Horror of the Heights

www.acblack.com

Text copyright © 2000 Anthony Masters
Illustrations copyright © 2000 Peter Dennis
Cover illustration copyright © 2008 Anthony Williams

The rights of Anthony Masters and Peter Dennis to be
identified as author and illustrator of this work respectively
have been asserted by them in accordance with the
Copyrights, Designs and Patents Act 1988.

ISBN 978-0-7136-8624-1

A CIP catalogue for this book is available
from the British Library.

This book is produced using paper that is made from wood
grown in managed, sustainable forests. It is natural, renewable and
recyclable. The logging and manufacturing processes conform to
the environmental regulations of the country of origin.

Printed and bound in China by C&C Offset Printing.

The Horror of the Heights

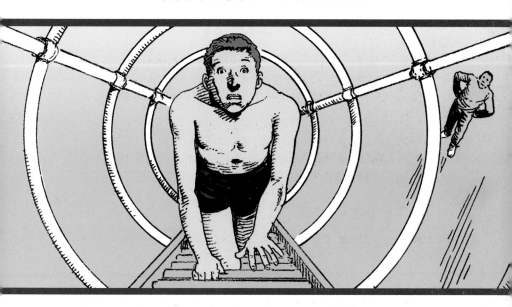

Anthony Masters
illustrated by Peter Dennis

A & C Black • London

Chapter One

Dean Lambert gazed up at the Horror of the Heights. That's what he had nicknamed the high diving board at the Wave Crest Leisure Centre. Now he was determined to conquer his fear.

Dean's dad, Luke Lambert, was the manager of the leisure centre. His older brother, Tim, was a champion diver. The two of them watched anxiously as Dean started to climb the ladder to the highest board.

Not daring to look down, Dean slowly climbed up, the fear of failing slightly worse than the fear of jumping.

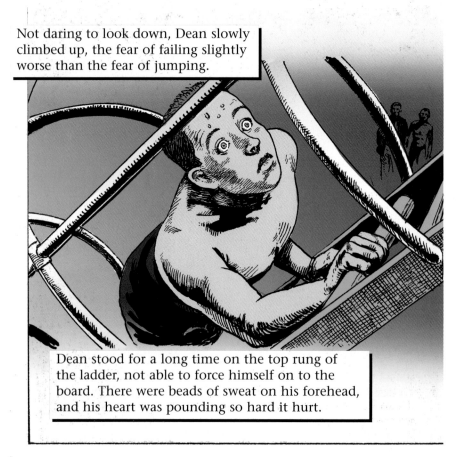

Dean stood for a long time on the top rung of the ladder, not able to force himself on to the board. There were beads of sweat on his forehead, and his heart was pounding so hard it hurt.

He glanced down, only to see his dad and Tim staring up at him, willing him on. They both so much wanted him to succeed.

You can do it, Dean.

But Dean knew he couldn't. He could never stand on that swaying board, staring down at the dark blue water below. It would be impossible.

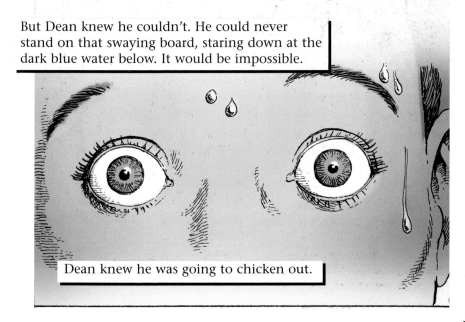

Dean knew he was going to chicken out.

Deeply ashamed, Dean slowly began to climb down. When he reached the side of the pool, his brother and father were waiting for him.

Bad luck. Next time, son.

Then his dad quickly walked away.

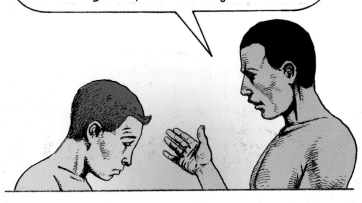

No way. It's just that the car crash is still bothering him. The other driver died in the accident, and Dad can't forgive himself, even though the police said it wasn't his fault.

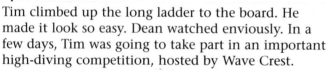

Tim climbed up the long ladder to the board. He made it look so easy. Dean watched enviously. In a few days, Tim was going to take part in an important high-diving competition, hosted by Wave Crest.

Tim stood on the board and waved down at Dean. He then took a run, prepared to dive…

...suddenly, the board collapsed, making him fall awkwardly down into the pool, catching his ankle on the springboard below.

Without thinking, Dean jumped after him into the diving pool – even though he hated being out of his depth. He was a fast swimmer though, and he soon reached Tim, who was floating on his back, sputtering. Tim was grinning, even though he was in pain.

It's lucky you didn't step on that board, isn't it?

You OK?

12

Tim hauled himself up on the side of the pool, and Dean followed.

Wait a minute. You were out of your depth back there.

So?

Tim put his arm around Dean's shoulders.

You did that for me, didn't you?

What if I did?

Mr Lambert inspected the board.

A bolt's loose! I'm going to get Ken.

He went off to find Ken Drake, the centre's maintenance man, as well as the swimming coach.

That's weird, isn't it? Ken inspects all the equipment every day. How could he have miss that?

Maybe the bolt suddenly worked loose.

Tim looked worried.

It doesn't happen like that.

Chapter Two

The next day, Ken and Mr Lambert were putting some of the young divers through their paces, including Ben Robinson, Tim's closest rival.

Dean decided to watch, still worried about his brother's ankle. But the bruising didn't seem to bother Tim as he took his turn and dived from the top board.

Ken was encouraging. Mr Lambert wasn't. He was yelling at his son.

Come on, Tim! What are you doing? That's no good! You can't afford to be off form. The competition's in a couple of days.

Dean noticed that Ben was watching Tim closely, no doubt enjoying hearing him criticised. Dean had never liked Ben. He had a huge ego and was a poor loser.

At the end of the session, Dean was even more worried as he overheard a fight between his dad and Ken. They were shouting at each other so loudly it was impossible not to hear them.

You're pushing Tim too hard! You'll break him. He'll lose all his confidence.

Nonsense! He's not working hard enough.

Who's the coach around here? You or me?

You're too soft.

Ken walked away towards the changing rooms.
The few divers still practising looked awkward
and embarrassed. And one of them was Tim.

Chapter Three

There was a pool-side disco that evening to celebrate the opening of Raging Waters, the new water slides at the leisure centre. Swimmers entered the three slides, plunged through twisting tubes on streams of water, and tumbled into a pool at the bottom.

Tim and Dean went with Maggie and Dawn, two of the Wave Crest lifeguards.

The slides were a popular new attraction. Long queues of people waited to try them.

Dean and Maggie were dancing together when they heard a scream and cries of pain coming from the pool.

They raced over to see a boy clambering out with a badly cut arm. The boy's father was already there. So was Luke Lambert. He looked horrified.

Luke kept apologising to the father while an attendant dried the boy's arm and applied first aid.

Later that night, the investigation began as the staff stripped away the plastic sides of the Twister, the slide that had injured the boy.

Look at this! This panel's been taken out and someone's roughed up the inside edge with a knife.

First the board and now the slide. Maybe we're being sabotaged!

Afterwards, Dean and Maggie walked home through the dark, winter streets. Dean liked Maggie a lot. She was funny and pretty, and she seemed to like him, too. She was the first girl who hadn't treated him like a kid.

At the moment, Dean had other things on his mind. He was not only worried about Wave Crest, but Tim, too. What if another piece of equipment collapsed on him?

Then there was his dad to consider. He'd been so quiet since the car crash, but also mean and bad tempered. These accidents at Wave Crest weren't going to bring back the old Dad, who was kind and generous and fun to be with.

Dean could see how scared she was.
He didn't feel that good himself.

Chapter Four

The leisure centre was eerie without its customers. All Dean and Maggie could hear from their hiding place in the storeroom the next night was the clanking of the air vents and the gurgling of water in the pools. Maggie grabbed Dean's shoulder.

I think I can hear someone moving.

But when they reached the gloom of the diving pool, lit only by a couple of security lights, neither Maggie nor Dean could see anything that looked suspicious.

Who's got keys besides your dad?

Only Ken Drake.

They don't like each other, do they?

Dean felt defensive about his father.

What do you mean?

Didn't they have a row recently?
One of many?

It's not that bad.

Isn't it?

Chapter Five

The next day, Mr Lambert was furious when he heard a rumour about what Dean and Maggie had done.

You two ought to be thoroughly ashamed of yourselves.

We wanted to catch whoever was sabotaging things. It was my idea –

I'm sure it was. Only you could be stupid enought to pull a stunt like that.

That evening, a large audience sat around the pool as the divers awaited the beginning of the competition. Dean and Maggie had good seats next to the high diving board. On the opposite side were Mr Lambert and Ken Drake, near the line of judges. All of the divers' supporters were there.

Then Dean's thoughts switched to the saboteur, and he glanced around at the spectators.

I wonder who did do the sabotage?

Some stupid vandal.

You'd need to know a lot about pool equipment. It has to be an insider.

Dawn passed by. Dean leaned over and whispered to her.

Has anyone been near the diving boards since they were last checked?

No one.

Unless you count Ken Drake, of course. I did see him making a few adjustments to the high diving board.

Dean was out of his mind with worry. The contestants were lining up now and he could see his brother was going to be the first to dive.

Hang on a minute!

What is it? We've only got a minute left!

Dean was no longer listening. He was edging along the row of seats and running to the side of the pool, hurrying towards his brother.

44

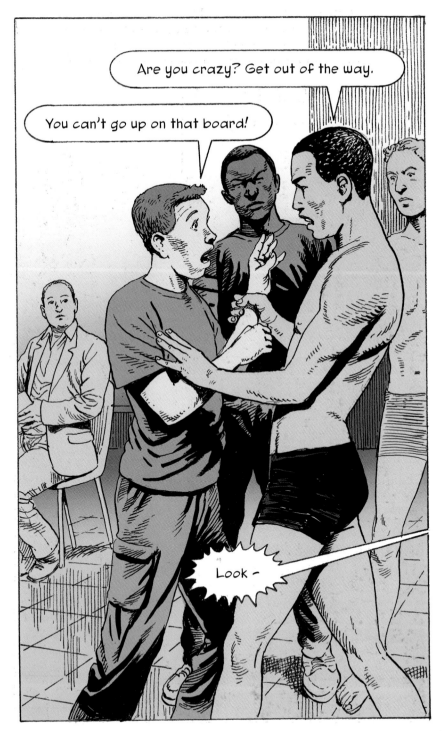

The audience was worried now. Some people were rising from their seats and asking questions that no one could answer. Their muttering grew to a roar.

The board could have been sabotaged in the last half hour.

Dean was so loud and upset that he sounded convincing.

I'll go and see.

Mr Lambert looked grim as he headed for the ladder. Dean noticed that Ken Drake was gazing up in alarm. The spectators were quiet now as his father carefully inspected the top board. Then his shoulders sagged and Dean knew with a sickening tug inside that he'd been right – there was something wrong.

What is it?

Mr Lambert quickly climbed down the ladder.

A bolt's been removed. Again!

Ken walked over, looking horrified.

Another one? I don't believe this.

He walked back to Maggie.

He briefly glanced down the side of the pool at Ben, who was looking devastated. Maggie paused uneasily.

Chapter Six

Dawn had moved over to the side of the pool and was leaning against the wall. Without waiting any longer, Dean began to run towards her, so wild with rage that he felt almost out of control. He could kill her. She could have killed his brother.

Dawn!

What is it?

Dawn gazed at him in amazement, but when she saw the murderous look in Dean's eyes, she cringed back in fear.

You did that, didn't you?

Dawn looked at him in shock.

The audience watched in amazement as she began to run along the side of the pool, hotly pursued by Dean.

Maggie was behind him now as Dean chased Dawn out of the diving area and into the main complex. The evening swimming session was almost over. The slides were closing, and most people were heading for the showers.

Dawn was heading for the slides, but as she ran up the ramp, she tripped and fell.

Although she got back on her feet fast, Dean knew that the gap between them had narrowed.

Dean and Maggie were only a metre behind Dawn now and he felt a wild surge of triumph as he realised she couldn't escape. Then one of the attendants called to Dawn.

As she plunged in head-first, the attendant gasped.

One moment Dawn was there. The next moment she wasn't. Dean gave an angry cry of rage. He turned back to Maggie.

Grab her when she comes out into the pool.

What's going on? Is this a charity stunt or something? Mr Lambert should have...

But Dean wasn't listening. Instead, wearing his T-shirt, jeans, and trainers, he followed Dawn down the swirling waters of the Twister.

Fully dressed, the ride down was very uncomfortable as Dean was whipped from one side to another, as the slide carried him through twisting corners and sudden drops. Soaked and gasping, he was finally flung into the pool.

When Dean surfaced, he could see Dawn and Maggie struggling together in the shallow end.

What's the matter with you two? I haven't done anything. I haven't done anything at all.

She was crying now and no longer trying to wrench herself out of Maggie's grip.

As Dean staggered towards them in his wet clothes, weighed down by his dripping trainers, a faint cheer went up from the spectators.

They must be doing it for charity. It's amazing what young people will do these days.

Mr Lambert was staring at the bedraggled threesome, still wading in the pool while the crowd grew larger around them.

What do you think you're doing? Get out of there! Now!

She stood there silently, staring at Dean, and suddenly he knew. There was something in her look. Something that told him everything. But why?

Shivering and draped in towels, Dean, Maggie, and Dawn sat in Mr Lambert's office, drinking tea they didn't want. Luke was shocked.

You hated me that much?

My father was everything to me.

It wasn't Dad's fault.

But your dad's still alive. Mine's not! I couldn't stand that. So I came to work here at Wave Crest. I wanted to learn the ropes...

65

Dean's rage surfaced again.

Chapter Seven

The next morning, Dean and Tim walked toward the high diving board. The pool was closed, and no one else was around.

OK?

I'm scared.

But this time you're going to jump.

I'm going to try.

You're going to succeed.

As Dean began to climb the ladder, hands and knees shaking, he tried to distract himself by thinking about what his dad had done for Maggie. He still couldn't believe his father had let her off, knowing what she had done and how much she hated him.

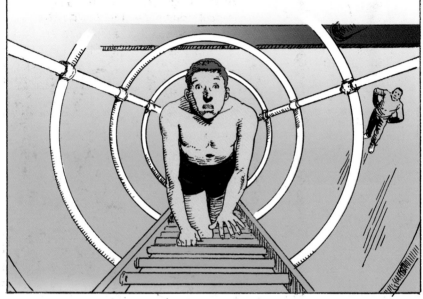

Tim broke into his thoughts.

Go for it! It's going to be OK!

Dean's breath was coming in little gasps and sweat was pouring down his face, but his father's words still rang in his ears.

What I'm going to do, Maggie, is call your mum and suggest we three all have a chat. You need some help.

Dean hadn't heard his father talk like that for ages. In fact, ever since Maggie had made her confession, Dad seemed to have become his old self again.

Dean was shaking as he reached the Horror of the Heights. When he got to the top rung of the ladder, Dean froze. This was where he had failed before.

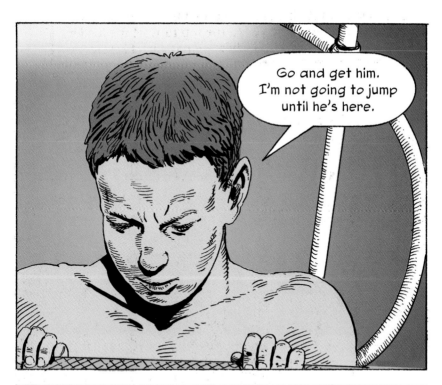

Tim ran out and returned almost immediately with their father. Dean realised he must have been waiting somewhere nearby.

Luke Lambert strolled towards him.

I'm here now. Go for it!

His dad made it sound as if the jump would be easy.

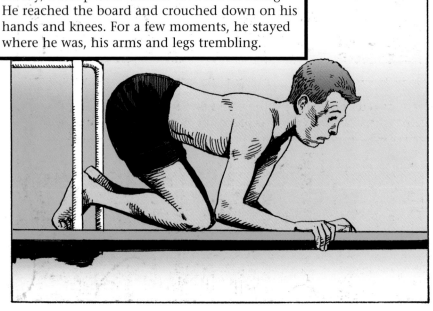

Slowly, Dean pulled himself over the last rung. He reached the board and crouched down on his hands and knees. For a few moments, he stayed where he was, his arms and legs trembling.

The dark blue water below looked cruel and distant. Suppose he jumped wrong? Would he hit the side of the pool and break his arms and legs? Would he break his neck and die a painful death or be crippled for life?

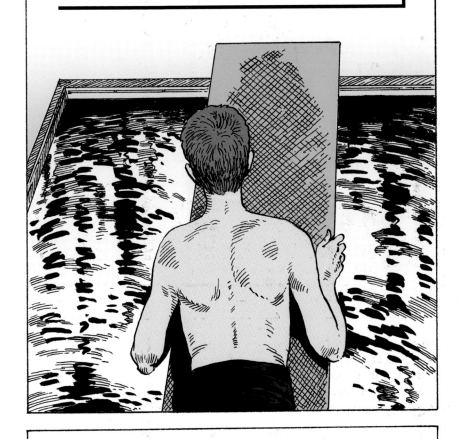

Dean looked down at his father, who was now leaning against the wall. Only Tim seemed nervous as he gazed up.

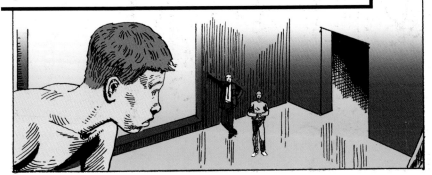

Dean tried to get to his feet, but his arms and legs felt like jelly. He stayed crouching, smelling the chlorine, and listening to the water sloshing against the sides of the pool.

Dean wiped away the sweat from his eyes and struggled to his feet.

Then the kind words his father had spoken to Maggie drained his fear away. "I told you – you need some help. Let's sort it out with your mother. Try not to hate me any more."

"I don't," Maggie had sobbed. "I really don't."

Dean staggered to the edge of the board. There seemed to be a roaring in his ears and, for a moment, he almost overbalanced.

Then he slowly lifted his arms. The board was swaying. So was he. Dean jumped!

He landed in the pool with an enormous splash, and relief soared in him, so much he felt light-headed.

Dad and Tim were leaping about, clapping and cheering, and suddenly Dean had never felt so happy in his life.

Then, to his amazement, he realised he was swimming comfortably in deep water. Dean was out of his depth, but he didn't mind.

He swam over to his father and brother. They each grabbed an arm and triumphantly pulled him out of the pool.

Tim thumped him on the back so hard it hurt.

Dean ran towards the ladder and began to climb up to the Horror of the Heights. But it wasn't horrifying any more.

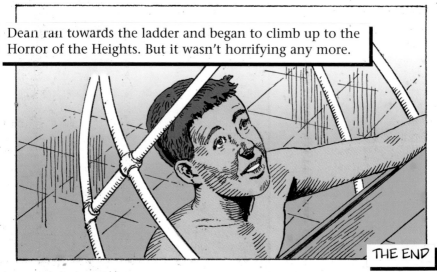

80